The FIRST BOOK of
The Spanish-American West

The FIRST BOOK of

The Spanish-American West

HENRY CASTOR

Illustrated by Albert Micale

*Franklin Watts, Inc. 575 Lexington Avenue
New York 22*

FIRST PRINTING
Library of Congress Catalog Card Number 63–16911
© Copyright 1963 by Franklin Watts, Inc.
Printed in the United States of America

A los amigos de mi alma en el oeste hispanoamericano, y especialmente los que viven en California

Contents

The FIRST BOOK of
The Spanish-American West

The Land and the Indians

The Land

PRAIRIE and plateau, mountain and desert—vast stretches of the American West once were Spanish. These lands are varied in appearance, but they all have one thing in common. They are the driest section of the United States.

The great mass of this dry country lies west of the 100th meridian of longitude and south of the 42nd parallel of latitude. The 100th meridian (shown on the map, pages 2-3) is the eastern boundary of the Texas Panhandle, while the 42nd parallel

1

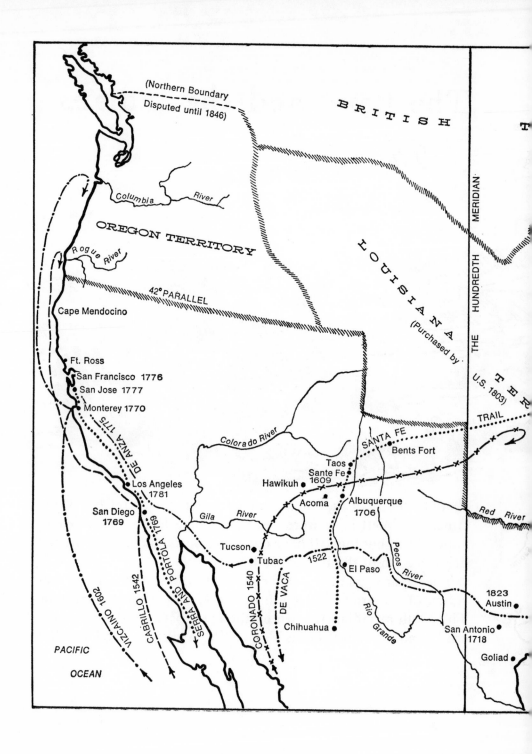

THE UNITED STATES AND THE SPANISH WEST BEFORE 1846

ERRITORY

MICHIGAN 1805

TERRITORY

MAINE 1820

VT 1791

N.H.

MASS.

CONN.

R.I.

NEW YORK

42° PARALLEL

PENNSYLVANIA

N.J.

STATES

OHIO 1803

DEL.

ILLINOIS 1818

INDIANA 1816

VIRGINIA

Westport

St. Louis

KENTUCKY 1792

Independence

NORTH CAROLINA

THIRTEEN

TENNESSEE 1796

SOUTH CAROLINA

THE ORIGINAL

RITORY

Mississippi River

ALABAMA 1819

GEORGIA

ATLANTIC OCEAN

MISSISSIPPI 1817

Sabine River

San Jacinto 1836

New Orleans (De Bienville 1718)

FLORIDA 1819

Ft. Anahuac

. St. Louis
a Salle 1685)·

·GULF OF MEXICO

is the northern boundary of California, Nevada, and part of Utah. In any normal year, outside the Pacific Coast area, only 14 inches of rain falls on the Spanish-American West. By contrast, New England gets about 40 inches annually.

The high mountains of the West block off rain clouds carried from the Pacific by the prevailing westerly winds. Eastward of these "Shining Mountains," deserts, stony plateaus, and treeless prairies stretch from Mexico into Canada. Not too long ago, schoolchildren were taught to call the Southwest "the Great

American Desert." It is an often spectacular place of petrified forests and brightly colored, or "painted," deserts, of sandstorms and flash floods, of mirages and disappearing rivers. Peculiar animals live there: among others, a rattlesnake that travels by throwing its body sideways in a series of loops, and so is called a "sidewinder," and a rather comical bird that can fly but prefers to run, and so has been named a "roadrunner."

In dry country, extremes of temperature are ordinary. Old-timers of the Texas Panhandle used to say that in winter nothing

but a couple of strands of rusty barbed wire shielded them against blasts from the North Pole. Yet in summer the thermometers of the West usually run higher than elsewhere in the United States.

California usually gets heavy winter rains, but is dry in the summer. Some of the rain clouds are checked by the Sierra Nevada mountain range, the "Snowy Sawteeth," and modern dams and reservoirs hold back the snow water for California's summer needs. Yet at one point the fertile San Joaquin Valley is only a hundred miles from Death Valley, the lowest, hottest, driest place in America. The "Snowy Sawteeth" are the wall that keeps Death Valley dry.

Animal and plant life in the Spanish-American West, as else-

6

where, vary according to rainfall and altitude. The cactus is a symbol of the desert. The piñon pine likes the high plateaus. The redwood grows on the west slopes of the Coast Range, and nowhere else in the world. A cousin of the redwood, the sequoia, is the most massive tree in the world, but a gnarled little tree of the southern Sierras, the bristlecone pine, has taken over the title of "the oldest living thing on earth." One of these trees is 4,600 years old.

For the United States west of the 100th meridian, guidebooks to birds, flowers, and trees are quite different from those for the remainder of the country. Different, too, were the Indians of the West from the Algonquin and Iroquois of the eastern forests.

The Indians

THE copper-skinned people whom the Spaniards found in the Americas ranged from the civilized Aztecs and Incas to types who ate ants and occasionally one another. On the Great Plains west of the Mississippi they were nomads, enjoying territory within limits set by continual and traditional wars. From the Blackfeet and Sioux of the north to the Apache and Comanche of the south, these were the fiercest warriors of North America. The rumbling buffalo herds which roamed the prairies made the Plains Indians mighty.

The bison (often called buffalo) is a kind of ox. If he is no stupider than an ox, he is no brighter, either. Even on foot, In-

dians killed these animals by disguising themselves as buffalo
and mingling with a herd. Women could stampede the beasts
over the edge of a cliff by screaming and waving their arms.

No tribe ever wasted the results of such slaughter. Hides,
meat, bones, and sinews were all useful as clothing, food, tools,
and cordage. Only the white man could, in fifty years (1850-
1900), almost wipe out a beast whose greatest numbers have been
estimated at from 60 to 500 million. The end of the buffalo was
the downfall of the Plains Indian. And most of the deliberate
butchery fattened only coyotes and buzzards.

11

Natives who did not roam with the buffalo herds worked settled farms, as the Navajo did. Some lived in cliffside apartment buildings, as the Pueblos did. But, despite regional differences and tribal habits, the Indians of the Spanish-American West were all alike in one respect. A tribe shared and shared alike in the goods of the land. That a white man would even go so far as to kill somebody to keep wealth for his own private use puzzled and disgusted all the Indians.

The Coming of the Spaniards

Los Conquistadores

FOR centuries the Roman Catholic soldiers of Spain had practiced the arts of war against the Moslem Moors from Africa, invaders of their land. But in 1492, just before the discovery of America, Spanish swordsmen finally succeeded in driving out the last of the invading Moors. Now, with foreign enemies no longer near at hand, the veteran Spanish warriors turned to conquests abroad.

The New World offered a worthy battleground for the Dons, or knights and noblemen. Not only did the Americas promise elbowroom for good fighting, but they also held out hope of riches. Besides, their native Indians were heathen who, the Spanish felt, should be converted to Christianity. So "Gold, God, and Glory" became the dream of the Dons, and to be conquerors became their duty. *Los conquistadores,* as they were called, wrecked the Indian empires and made slaves of their peoples.

The Dons were a lone and quarrelsome sort of men, at times united with their fellows only by their Catholic faith. To fill their wallets they relied, not on trades or farming, but on their swords. They rarely took their wives on their travels. Even later, as settled ranchers in New Spain (as Mexico was called), the Dons remained *gachupines,* "spur-wearers," brave, cruel, and pious.

For over four hundred years (1492-1898) the Spaniards ruled vast territories in the Americas. Today the former domain of

the Spanish Crown in the American West covers all of California, Texas, Arizona, New Mexico, Nevada, and Utah, as well as parts of Colorado, Oklahoma, Wyoming, and Kansas. In addition, the Spanish king once ruled Florida and the Louisiana Territory. In this book, however, we shall talk chiefly about the West, the "Land of Little Rain," the "Land of Shining Mountains."

Cow Head Came First

CABEZA DE VACA never intended to tour Texas. One of an unlucky band of *conquistadores* from Florida led by Pánfilo de Narváez, he was shipwrecked near today's Galveston in 1528. Cabeza de Vaca means "Cow Head," but his deeds proved more of the man than his name suggests.

The Indians who captured him discovered that he could heal their sick by prayer and touch. But Cabeza de Vaca himself felt uneasy about his gift; he thought his Church might frown on his miraculous cures.

In time, his captors trusted him to journey inland as their agent, trading seashells for dyes, and arrow-cane for skins. He always returned, to stand by a sick fellow-Spaniard until both should have a chance to escape. Eventually Cabeza de Vaca wandered across Texas, and west clear to the Gulf of California, picking up other Narváez survivors on the way. "Cow Head" was the first European to cross the Continental Divide from eastern salt water to western.

He was also the first European to see buffalo and eat their

16

meat. To him the bison were "humpbacked cattle." Usually Cabeza de Vaca and his friends were hungry, however, and they went naked even in winter. But at last Cabeza de Vaca's mystic talent as a medicine man made their journey like a parade, with hordes of adoring Indians passing him along from tribe to tribe.

In the summer of 1536, four sun-blackened, shaggy men— all who were left of Narváez's original four hundred—plodded into Mexico, where there were already Spaniards. Cabeza de Vaca had never doubted that God would bring him home.

Religious faith was one of Cabeza de Vaca's marks as a Christian, but he did not share another displayed by the Spaniards who found him. To his intense disgust they enslaved the trusting Indians who were his escort. His tolerance of red men even landed him in jail, for this trait was suspiciously unlike normal *conquistador* arrogance.

Álvar Núñez Cabeza de Vaca died in Spain, unknown and unhonored. But he had honored Spain.

The Golden Knight in Cibola

ONE of Cabeza de Vaca's companions in misery had been a Moor called Estéban. In 1539 he guided a Catholic friar, Marcos de Niza, north from New Spain (Mexico) to see the Seven Cities of Cibola. Indian rumor said that gold and jewels were so common in Cibola that people stuck them in pavements and walls. But Estéban was killed by Zuñi Indians, and Fray, "Friar," Marcos had to retreat.

Niza did view the cliff-hanging towns of the Pueblo Indians

from a distance, however. The mountain air must have played tricks with his eyes, for the friar reported that Cibola was greater than Tenochtitlán, the glorious capital of Montezuma, emperor of the Aztecs, had ever been.

The news excited Francisco Vásquez de Coronado, a provincial governor. Within a year he set out to conquer the fabulous cities. Don Francisco's golden armor glinted in the hot sun as he watched the march-out from Compostela, a town near the Pacific where Cabeza de Vaca had ended his odyssey. Coro-

20

nado's guns rumbled, his Indian allies howled, his hundreds of Spanish troops clattered. Herds of livestock kicked up clouds of dust. Three small ships paralleled the march, sailing up the Gulf of California into the Colorado River.

Coronado, the Golden Knight, impatiently pushed ahead of the column with a hundred men, including Fray Marcos. After two months of dusty riding he approached Hawikuh, one of the Seven Cities. Hawikuh was a thumping letdown—nothing but "a little, crowded village, looking as if it had been all crumpled together." A brisk fight won the town, but Coronado was

wounded. Nobody found gold. Niza was cursed and packed off home in disgrace.

Another wing of Don Francisco's army made contact with its fleet on the Colorado, and met giant Yuma Indians. Some others stared into the Grand Canyon in awe. "Rocks on the sides of the cliffs seemed to be as tall as a man, but those who went down swore that when they reached those rocks they were bigger than the great tower of Seville."

Still another lieutenant, Hernando de Alvarado, saw one of the oldest dwelling places in America, Acoma. Perched on a seventy-acre table of white rock, it lifted 350 feet above the plain, west of present-day Albuquerque, New Mexico. Don Hernando passed on to the Rio Grande and Pecos river valleys, and far enough east to glimpse buffalo.

In winter quarters, Coronado heard from an Indian that in the land called Gran Quivira cheap gold was cast into bells and ships' prows. No Spaniard ever failed to act on Indian romances about gold, but before he went forth Don Francisco humbled the Indians in his vicinity. His treacherous winter slaughter, by sword and fire, left bitter memories of the white men, never forgotten by the Indians.

Coronado's diminished army struck off across the *Llano Estacado,* the "Staked Plain," so named by the Spanish because of the many stalks of yucca plant that grew in the region. The soldiers were depressed by the land, flat and dull to all horizons under a bowl of burning sky. After weeks of thirsty marching they became suspicious of the Indian who had boasted of Quivira, and Don Francisco had him strangled. Gran Quivira is now known as Kansas. Somewhere there the Golden Knight erected a cross, on which he wrote, "Coronado reached this place."

23

Footsore and angry, the troops turned back. They wintered near today's Taos, New Mexico, fighting among themselves and vowing to go home. A handful of Catholic friars led by Juan Padilla bravely remained behind to convert the Indians. Most of them, including Fray Juan, were martyred. Coronado must be blamed for their deaths. He had demonstrated to the red men that white men could not be trusted.

A scant hundred tattered Spaniards got back to New Spain

24

in 1542. Most of what they left behind vanished forever in the wilderness, but not their cows and horses. Their Spanish Andalusian cattle increased to millions on the southern plains, and in time became the famous longhorns of Texas. Their lost horses fathered the wild mustangs that enriched the lives of the Indians who caught and tamed them. Before the Golden Knight passed by, no western Indian had ever seen a horse. After Coronado's going, the mustangs made the Indians swifter as buffalo hunters, and so assured their families plenty of meat. A tribe's wealth was counted in horses; wars were fought for them; brides were bought with them. In a few generations the little mustangs transformed one tribe, the Ute, from lowly hillbillies to one of the most dashing bands of the plains.

Sea Dogs and Amazons

CALIFORNIA, realm of black women-warriors led by a queen flashing a sword of gold, was a fiction created by a Spanish novelist in 1510. Montalvo may have borrowed the name from the ancient Song of Roland, where it appears as "Califerne."

Hernando Cortes, conqueror of Montezuma, heard rumors of just such a land of Amazons to the north, "very close to the side of the Terrestrial Paradise." He sent men to find it. The Dons of New Spain were beginning to believe their own fables. Their king was so annoyed that he forbade them to read any more novels.

In 1533 one of Cortes' men discovered a "pearl-bearing island" which Cortes named California. Six years later, Fran-

cisco de Ulloa sailed around the coasts of Baja, "Lower," California, hunting the Strait of Anian, which was supposed to connect the Pacific with the Atlantic. He guessed Lower California to be a peninsula.

The earliest coastal explorer of Alta, "Upper," or American, California was a Portuguese-born sea dog named Juan Rodríguez Cabrillo. In 1542, Don Juan hoisted sail on two leaky ships and found the Bay of San Diego, fortunately just before a storm. Farther north he named another harbor the Bay of Smokes for the Indian fires he saw; now it is Santa Monica Bay, near Los Angeles. Past Catalina and the Channel Islands Cabrillo coasted, on past Monterey Bay and the Golden Gate, neither of which he saw for fog.

In January, 1543, Cabrillo died after two months in agony with a broken shoulder, but he told his pilot to carry on. Bartolemé Ferrelo did so, locating Cape Mendocino and possibly reaching the mouth of the Rogue River in Oregon before he turned back.

In the same year, the Philippine Islands were linked to New Spain by an expedition commanded by López de Villalobos, but a sea-going priest made the Manila run practical. In 1564, Andrés de Urdaneta discovered the Japan Current in the Pacific. Thereafter the treasure-laden Manila galleons used favorable sea currents both to and from the Orient, in a long triangle from Acapulco to Manila to Cape Mendocino in northern California, and thence back to Mexico.

The last notable sea search of the early days was led by a mere trader. But even if Sebastián Vizcaíno could not write "Don" before his name, he was a skilled captain. In an effort to locate a supply port for the use of the Manila galleons in Upper California, Vizcaíno found Monterey Bay in 1602. One of his ships probably looked into the mouth of a mythical "River of the West," which is now the Columbia.

San Francisco Bay kept its secret. Despite the daring of the Spanish sea dogs, the fogbound Golden Gate remained rumored but unknown for more than a century and a half after Vizcaíno.

Spain's near monopoly of the oceans ended abruptly in 1588. In a running battle with the English that lasted several days, she lost her great fighting fleet. The destruction of the Armada by English sailors and Irish storms crippled Spain. It also opened the seas to the rising colonial powers of Europe: England, France, and Holland. As their stars rose, that of Spain's began to flicker.

27

New Mexico and Arizona

IN 1598, Juan de Oñate invaded New Mexico at the head of a procession of splendidly dressed Dons, some of whom confidently had brought along their wives. Once again, hope of riches spurred their dreams. In 1581 a real gold strike had been made near what is now Prescott, Arizona.

But Oñate found no gold, and the friars with him turned pale at his brutalities. Don Juan killed, burned alive, or forced into slavery the entire population of Acoma, the ancient town on the white rock in the sky. In 1607 he was recalled by the Crown, and eventually was replaced by Pedro de Peralta, who founded a town in 1609, naming it Santa Fe. Next to St. Augustine, in Florida, founded by Spaniards in 1565, it is the oldest city in the United States.

Despite bloody Indian revolts, and despite isolation and sloth, New Mexico grew to be the most prosperous part of New Spain's northern domain. In 1706, Albuquerque was started by thirty-five families. By the 1820's the green Rio Grande Valley supported over forty thousand people, ten times as many as either Texas or California. The New Mexico of those days was much larger than the present-day state. Along with the area of modern New Mexico, it included that of Utah, Nevada, and parts of Colorado and Arizona.

The Indians did all the work of the settlements, were paid nothing, and were lashed regularly by their overseers, sometimes for fun. In the early days, New Mexico's economy was such that a sheep was worth a pair of shoes or a pound of chocolate, a priest might receive a string of chili peppers as payment for saying a Mass, and there was nothing unusual in a child's being swapped for a knife.

Arizona benefited by the missions and stock farms established by Fray Eusebio Kino, a tireless traveler. His exploration of the lower Colorado River proved Lower California to be a peninsula, and he produced a map of the country that was best

for a century. Kino loved Indians, but the ever hostile Apache irritated him. On one occasion he turned soldier, leading a scalp-taking raid of Pima against the troublesome Apache.

The energetic friar's monument today is the city of Tucson, in Arizona. In 1700 he built on its southern outskirts a church now in use, San Xavier del Bac.

The Missions

Soldiers and Priests

RUSSIANS prowling in the Pacific troubled King Carlos of Spain. The ships of Catherine the Great were searching for the mythical Strait of Anian. Russian seal and otter hunters had taken over the Aleutian Islands off Alaska. No Spanish outposts existed to prevent invaders from moving into New Spain.

José de Gálvez, agent for the king in Mexico, summoned two men to conference. In March, 1769, a familiar Spanish method of occupying new lands began once more. A joint force of soldiers under Gaspar de Portolá, and friars under Junípero Serra went north. By securing Upper California they meant to make Mexico safe. Priests were sent as comrades in conquest because they were cheaper for the king to keep than soldiers, and less likely to cause trouble. For themselves, the *frailes,* "friars," went forth because they believed deeply that pagan Indians must be converted wherever they were found.

Fray Junípero dedicated his first mission at San Diego, Cali-

fornia, on July 14, 1769. A master of the difficult Indian tongues, he preached to the first of his many converts, and gave them simple gifts before resuming the march with Don Gaspar. Fray Junípero really *marched;* he did not trust horses.

Both priests and soldiers thought the land looked forlorn. The rolling foothills and the valleys were dry, as always in summer, and the mountains looked "inaccessible not only to men but also to goats and deer." Portolá's horses and those of the Spaniards who followed, however, were to change one aspect of California's hills forever. The oats brought along for feed—and for crops which were planted later—very easily grew wild. To this day they make a covering on the hills, green in the winter and brown in the summer.

Don Gaspar's troops discovered the pits of slow-bubbling tar, *la brea,* at a place now within today's Los Angeles. Thousands of

31

the bones of trapped prehistoric animals have been dredged from the La Brea Pits.

Fray Junípero's friars named the *palos colorados,* "redwood trees," that they saw north of Monterey Bay, which they were seeking. The trail blazed by these Spaniards is followed closely today by U. S. Route 101, *El Camino Real,* "the King's Highway."

At first, the expedition missed the bay at Monterey, but in so doing they blundered across a far greater one, San Francisco Bay. One hundred and sixty-seven years after Vizcaíno had sailed by the fog-cloaked Golden Gate without seeing it, a party of Portolá's hunters topped a hill and gazed down in wonder at "the harbor of harbors." Seven years later, Serra was to honor his sixth mission and the huge landlocked bay with the name of

the founder of his missionary order, San Francisco de Asís. For gentle St. Francis of Assisi to go any farther, Fray Junípero joked, "He must have boats."

When the friar returned to report to Gálvez in New Spain, he had completed a tramp of 2,400 miles, and his mind buzzed with plans for missions all along the way.

"Junípero Serra's Rosary"

THE beads of Serra's "rosary" were twenty-one missions in California, nine founded by Fray Junípero himself, and the rest by Frailes Lasuen and Tapis. The last of the missions was located

at Sonoma, thirty miles north of San Francisco, in 1823, when the time of all missions was running out. At the Sonoma and San Rafael missions the Spaniards finally encountered Russians, who had been based at Fort Ross, fifty miles northwest, since 1811. The amiable Russians gave gifts to the friars. Fort Ross failed after a few years, and the Russians went home.

Mission Indians were virtual prisoners. They could not leave the missions, were forced to attend church, and were locked in at night. Their usual food was barley mush, although they grew a variety of crops and tended the missions' sheep and swine. Pun-

ishment was laid on them by soldiers with whips.

In their wild state, the Indians lived so primitively that Americans later called them "Diggers," from their crude digging sticks. There were many tribes and languages, but none cultivated crops, or built tight shelters, or developed the handicrafts of eastern Indians. They ate fish, grasshoppers, and acorn bread; an occasional stranded whale was a great treat. In the missions they learned crafts, and sheltered warm and dry. They were made to work, to wear some clothes, and to display their rosaries, which the Indians thought were pretty.

Prisoners or not, most mission Indians came to love their gray-robed *padres* like real fathers. The friars worked beside them and, like Serra, lived very simply. Fray Junípero died quietly at Mission San Carlos in Carmel, on the bare boards that had been his only bed for years. He is buried there.

Inside a Mission

New Mexico had more missions than California, and there were others in Arizona and Texas. Most of them were older than Fray Junípero's, and one, the Alamo at San Antonio, in Texas, became the freedom shrine of a great state. But wherever they were planted, the missions looked much alike. Their architecture and furniture, as designed by the Franciscan friars, remain one continuing feature of the American West today.

Mission buildings were made of adobe bricks, poured as mud into blocks 5 × 11 × 22 inches, and set in the sun to harden. Lime mortar cemented them together; along the coast this often consisted of the powdered shells of a big local mollusk, the aba-

lone. Mission roofs were covered with curved red tiles. At first, to give them their rounded shape, the Indian masons fashioned these tiles by plastering adobe against the curve of their thighs.

If an adobe house kept a snug roof, pelting winter rains did it little harm. But if the dwelling were left alone, the adobe slowly returned to the earth that it was. Many missions vanished in this way, but some have been rebuilt from the old designs.

The adobe brick church, the friars' living quarters, the shops and storerooms were grouped around a *patio,* "courtyard," which had gardens and pools. Ruined San Juan Capistrano still keeps gardens to welcome back its punctual swallows, which return every March 19.

Often a high adobe or stone wall made a mission a fort, like the Texas Alamo. Inside, besides the buildings, were a water supply, a cemetery, and vegetable gardens. Indians tended to everything and, once they had been taught, became adept at weaving, carpentry, masonry, and carving. The friars who were their instructors had all these skills and many more. Mission San Lúis Rey, at Oceanside, the biggest of the California missions, even had a native band of forty pieces that played in the cool of the evening.

Today, Santa Barbara is the best preserved of the missions, and is the only one where Franciscans have served continuously from the beginning. Others, like San Lúis Rey and Santa Clara, have become schools; some, like San Diego, are museums; and two, at Lompoc and Sonoma, are state owned.

Death of the Missions

IT was not foreigners from Russia, England, or the United States who broke Fray Junípero's "rosary." The missions were overthrown by the Republic of Mexico after 1821.

When Mexico revolted against Spain, some friars armed their

mission Indians and drilled them to defend the land for the king. This action offended the Mexican patriots. Except for Padre Miguel Hidalgo, who had started the Wars of Mexican Independence in 1810, the patriots regarded the Catholic priests as untrustworthy royalists. Along with the army officers, they belonged to the hated privileged class called *gachupines,* or "spur-wearers."

Accordingly, the free government of Mexico abolished the missions and gave the property to the Indians. The simple red men did not understand that they were supposed to be responsible citizens of a new nation, however. They feared that the government was turning them out along with their trusted Franciscan fathers. In some cases the result was unhappy; the angry Indians wantonly destroyed the very herds, crops, and houses meant to be their own.

Mexico tried to sell the vacant mission properties, and the Indians were forced to return to the life they had led before Fray Junípero had walked among them, saying, *"Amar a Dios,"* or "Love God." They were bewildered, and probably less able to get along on their own than if they never had seen missions.

In 1846, American troopers, then at war with Mexico, stabled their horses in echoing San Diego, Fray Junípero's first mission. Other missions were used as barns; some were lost forever to silence and the weather. But in their short career, the California missions achieved important things for New Spain. They fended off the Russians. As inns, situated about forty miles apart, they made travel easier. They planted a community of Spaniards and Mexicans in a country destined for importance. And perhaps also they uplifted the thirty thousand Indians they served.

Not until the United States took over the Spanish West in 1848

40

did the Roman Catholic Church partly regain its own. The government restored some land to it, but kept most as federal property. What was left of the mission buildings after years of neglect also was returned to the Church. The Indians gained nothing.

The Incredible John the Baptist

IN the Spanish days, ships could carry colonists and supplies to Upper California, but an overland trail from the interior of Mexico was desirable. The man who established such a trail was Juan Bautista de Anza, who in 1774 picked his way across the Sierra Nevada from Tubac—in what is now Arizona—to the vicinity of present-day Los Angeles.

"John the Baptist" de Anza was a gay man and, except for the priests, was the outstanding leader of the mission period. In 1775 he again crossed the Continental Divide—this time on a journey that was not duplicated until the days of the forty-niners. He started out with 240 people and their livestock, to build a *presidio,* "fort," at San Francisco. Before the party lay more than a thousand miles of desert, and the horrors of mountain blizzards, Apache ambushes, lost herds, hunger, disease, and earthquakes. But the incredible Anza finished his trip with more people than he had to start. Several babies were born along the way. "John the Baptist" as a scout and wagon-train captain matches any man in North American history.

Anza's trail was useless after the once friendly Yuma massacred the Spanish outpost at the junction of the Gila and Colorado rivers. One of the slain, Fray Francisco Garcés, had been an early companion of Anza's, and himself had pioneered a route followed into Los Angeles many years later by the Santa Fe Railroad.

Anza's *presidio* by San Francisco Bay raised its flag in September, 1776. Far to the east in Philadelphia, the Declaration of Independence had been signed on the Fourth of July of that same year. Hence, San Francisco was born with the American nation. The civilian town, or *pueblo,* which grew up near the *presidio* and mission was not called San Francisco at first, however. It was named Yerba Buena, "good herb," after the wild mint that scented its hills.

Don Felipe de Neve started the first *pueblo* in California at San Jose in 1777. San Jose looked promising from the start, but nobody hoped for much from the forty-four nondescript Mexicans, male and female, who began the second civilian town in 1781. This shabby place trumpeted its name as El Pueblo de Nuestra Señora la Reina de los Angeles de Porciuncula. Now it is called simply Los Angeles, and sometimes even "L.A."

Texans and Mexicans

The Vacant Land

TEXAS, like California, was an unwanted child of New Spain. Neither of these two places seemed promising, and the Spaniards had to force or bribe people to settle in them. But the locations were strategic for protecting the Mexican heartland: California

44

was a shock absorber against the Russians, and Texas against the French.

About a century and a half after Cabeza de Vaca's pilgrimage across Texas, the rulers at Mexico City had awaked to a danger from the northeast. Frenchmen under Robert, Sieur de La Salle, had landed in east Texas in 1684. La Salle was the brilliant explorer who had claimed and named for his king the Louisiana Territory, the lands drained by the Mississippi and Missouri rivers.

La Salle was murdered by his own men, and his settlement failed. But its warning was clear. If New Spain could not fill the vacuum of Texas, France or England would. In an attempt to prevent this, the red and gold banner of Spain was hoisted in 1690 near an Indian village on the Neches River, and a mission was built and called San Francisco. Three soldiers and three priests manned Spain's tiny outpost in the vacant land.

In the years that followed, forts and counter-forts were built around the shores of the Gulf of Mexico, until in 1718 the French under the Sieur de Bienville founded the most famous, New Orleans. A few months before, the Spaniards had started their first civilian town inside Texas—San Antonio. By the end of 1721, Texas seemed snug in control of the governor of Coahuila, the Marquis de Aguayo. He had sponsored ten missions, four forts, and four struggling towns.

The competition ended peculiarly. In 1762, Louis XV of France gave Carlos III of Spain the whole realm of the Louisiana Territory. Carlos wasn't sure he wanted it. Spain was bone-tired; she had been mauled by a hundred years of European wars. But when England's Yankee colonies revolted in 1775, Spain seized a chance to damage one of her Old World rivals.

46

She became an ally of the infant United States. Spaniards wiped out British outposts on the Mississippi in 1779, and skirmished with the redcoats as far north as St. Joseph, Michigan.

In 1800, France regained the huge Louisiana Territory as part of a deal among the European powers. But only three years later, Napoleon Bonaparte sold it cheap to American President Thomas Jefferson. New Spain now had a frisky neighbor, the young United States of America.

Backwoodsmen and Empresarios

THE mischief that New Spain had suffered from European intruders on her claims was nothing compared to the grief that American frontiersmen gave her. They ignored Spanish laws forbidding travel, trapping, and trading. Once they trod on any part of an unknown country, their feet itched to feel the rest of it.

Since the Spanish government had failed to recruit European immigrants to mount guard in the Texas country, the Crown decided to employ Americans. This was like paying cats to become mice. After 1821 the Republic of Mexico continued the innocent plan, partly from gratitude for American volunteer help during the revolt from Spain.

Most of the early Texas pioneers were crude and leathery characters. But Stephen Austin, founder of a colony on the Brazos River, was a scholar and a fine flute player. Austin's agreement with the Mexican government was typical of all such

contracts. He swore to become a Mexican citizen and a Roman Catholic, and to bring in no less than a hundred families and no more than eight hundred in six years. In exchange, Mexico granted the *empresario,* "contractor," a vast tract of land, tax-free for seven years.

Besides restless backwoodsmen, the magnet of Texas drew from the States men who had been ruined by business panics. The *empresarios'* land was free, and easy to get to by wagon. And who knew what happy change of fortune might await a family there? The Mexicans welcomed the settlers as good people who would seal the door of their republic against United States aggression, and who also would help to tame the ferocious Apache and Comanche tribes.

Because of difficult communication, Mexico despaired of holding on to California and Arizona, but it hoped to keep Texas and New Mexico in hand.

Texans vs. Mexicans

ALMOST from the start there was bad blood between the colonists and their overlords. The cats could not become mice. The newcomers remained American and Protestant, regardless of their oaths to become Mexican and Catholic. Most of them were Southerners, and accepted slavery, which Mexico abolished. The colonists complained that they were not allowed proper representation at Mexico City, that there were no democratic elections, and that Mexican courts avoided jury trial. During the bickering, both sides showed the ignorant contempt for each other so often displayed by men of differing languages, customs, and religions.

Fighting started when Mexico set up garrisons among the Texans to police them. Curiously, the commander of the Mexicans at Fort Anahuac, who triggered the first shooting in 1832, was an American.

Mexico withdrew its troops. In 1833 the Texans sent Stephen Austin to urge General Antonio López de Santa Anna, new President of Mexico, to make Texas a province separate from Coahuila.

Santa Anna was a scoundrel whose betrayals of Texans were exceeded only by his treacheries toward his own people. He lived richly, and it amused him to carry fighting cocks with him everywhere. His vanity saw nothing absurd about holding cathedral ceremonies for a leg he lost in battle. Yet Santa Anna was so talented that time and again during his life his troubled country called him to leadership. Now, in 1833, he jailed Austin for his impudent request concerning Texas. And when Santa

Anna seized power as dictator in 1835, he again sent troops into Texas.

In 1835, the new Mexican garrison at Fort Anahuac was surprised into surrender by a small party of fire-eaters led by Colonel William B. Travis. Sensible colonists deplored the hasty action, but events were rushing out of control. Stephen Austin returned from two years in prison convinced that a war for independence had to come.

On November 14, 1835, a temporary rebel government was set up by the Texans, with Henry Smith as governor and Sam Houston as commander of the militia. Houston, a friend of Andrew Jackson, had once been governor of Tennessee, and at another time had been made a Cherokee chief called "the Raven."

51

"Remember the Alamo!"

ON February 25, 1836, a ten-day fight began. Colonel Travis and 187 men of Texas defended the Alamo, an abandoned walled mission in San Antonio. Four thousand besieging Mexicans wiped them out to the last man, and burned their bodies.

Travis's band included the legendary Davy Crockett, and

James Bowie, the inventor of a knife much used on the frontier. (As the Mexicans said, a bowie knife was "good either to open animals or close conversations.")

Other defenders of the Alamo came from a score of eastern states and foreign countries. Today all are honored as the first Texans. Jim Bowie was killed on his sickbed, still slashing with his knife. Such last-gasp resistance at the Alamo cost the lives of over fifteen hundred of Santa Anna's ill-fed, half-trained troops.

On March 27, Santa Anna won easily at Goliad. James Fannin had surrendered his 350 men to overwhelming odds, and the men were unarmed when the Mexicans murdered them.

The shambles at the Alamo and Goliad united the Texans, but some people felt panic when their general, Sam Houston, steadily retreated before the enemy. Would all of Texas fall to Santa Anna?

Big Sam bided his time. He wanted to collect more men and at the same time wear down the half-starved army of Mexicans. His tactics worked. On April 21, Sam's chance came at a marshy loop of the San Jacinto River, not far from today's city of Houston. Just as the army of 1,200 Mexicans was lying down for a noonday rest, a *siesta,* Sam attacked with his 783 men.

Charging under their new Lone Star flag and yelling, "Remember the Alamo!" the Texans annihilated their foes. Some terrified Mexicans cried out, "Me no Alamo," but half were slaughtered and the rest captured. Later, Santa Anna was released because he said that he would work for an independent Texas. Like most of his slippery promises, this one wasn't worth nine cents.

Fannin, Crockett, Bowie, Travis, and the others were avenged at San Jacinto. The Mexicans wanted no further fighting at this time, but they never would admit that Texas was a free nation.

The new republic held an election in October, 1836, and made Sam Houston its first President. The voters also agreed to join the United States promptly. But annexation was not simple. Ten years of bloodshed were to pass before the Lone Star flag was lowered in favor of the Stars and Stripes.

The Western Star

"Manifest Destiny"

THE United States more than doubled in area when it bought the Louisiana Territory in 1803 and Florida in 1819. Instead of satisfying the American appetite for growth, however, these increases only sharpened it. Feeling in the country was strongly "expansionist," desiring a spread of American power.

By Thomas Jefferson's orders the Lewis and Clark expedition had opened a trail into the Pacific Northwest that gave the United States a strong claim to the Oregon country, disputed by England. Both John Quincy Adams and Andrew Jackson tried to buy a part of Mexico. Politically, to be an expansionist was to attract votes, particularly from the midwestern and southern states. This fact was proved in 1844 by the election of the first "dark horse" (unexpected nominee) President, James K. Polk, who defeated the well-known Henry Clay because Clay hesitated to say he would seize territory. Polk had no such hesitations.

Reports from the glamorous West fanned the expansionist fever. Without much regard for accuracy, newspapers ran stories about the unknown lands, and traveling lecturers confirmed their wild tales. Sea captains brought back descriptions of a California climate so healthy that a man had to move away to die. Missionaries wrote from Oregon that they had found the Garden of Eden. And the first Texas brags began with the first Texans.

American desire for more land was not quite greed, however. Added to it was a sense of sacred duty about pushing back the frontier. Eventually a New York newspaper editor coined the phrase "manifest destiny" to justify America's westward expansion. "Manifest destiny" was the name given a belief that it was historically inevitable that a vigorous nation should spread out to its natural geographical boundaries. It was the "manifest destiny" of the United States, believers said, that a great ocean like the Pacific might stop the nation's growth, but nothing less could or should.

Someday, it was almost certain, the United States would be one country from ocean to ocean. No weary nation like Spain, or her revolution-torn heir, Mexico, could halt the Yankee push.

The Santa Fe Trail

AT the same time the *empresarios* were busy settling Texas, two other matters were deeply affecting "manifest destiny." The first was the opening of the earliest well-traveled route to the West, across the highlands of New Mexico.

So long as Spain had ruled the Rio Grande Valley, American traders and explorers who had ventured into the guarded area had been clapped into jail. One of those caught was a young army officer, Zebulon Pike, for whom Pike's Peak is named. In 1806 he was the first to describe the *pueblo* of Santa Fe for American readers.

With the birth of the Republic of Mexico, New Mexico's territory was thrown open to trade. By 1826, wagon trains over the Santa Fe Trail were making money for dealers in furs, gold, silver, and commoner merchandise. On the trail, Kit Carson and the Bent brothers, founders of Bent's Fort in Colorado, first became known. The trail's traffic interested important Americans like Thomas Hart Benton, senator from Missouri. Two towns in his state, Independence, and Westport (now part of Kansas City), were booming as the eastern ends of the trail. It ended at Los Angeles in the west, with a southern branch down to Chihuahua, Mexico.

But travelers on the Santa Fe Trail fought thirst, Indian raids, and death, and by 1843 the trade sputtered to a close because of clashes between Texans and Mexicans. The trail days had opened the eyes of many Americans, however. Overland travel had proved a practical way west. Experience had shown how wagon trains could band together to defy Indian attacks. Shrewd politicians like Senator Benton had caught a hint of how laxly Mexico held a tempting territory. American belief in "manifest destiny" was confirmed, since it was plain to believers that a weak Mexico did not deserve to own the land.

60

The Mountain Men

ALSO affecting "manifest destiny" were the mountain men. These few fierce scouts who roamed the high country of the west earned their fame between 1825 and 1840. They had "little fear of God and none of the devil," as they made tracks from the Mississippi to the Pacific and from Mexico to Canada, trapping animals, killing Indians—or sometimes marrying them—and walking in wilds no white man had ever known. Among the mountain men were Jed Smith, Joe Meek, Jim Beckwourth, and Jim Bridger.

The mountain men out-Indianed the Indian. They bore the tortures of hot alkali deserts and icy canyons without flinching. And few things going on about them escaped their attention, for inattention might mean death. A mountain man could travel for days, eating snakes and his own shoes, but he could put away nine pounds of meat at a sitting if he had it. Any savagery an Indian could think up, a mountain man could go one better. Yet, over a campfire a few could argue sensibly about Shakespeare's *Hamlet*.

These skin-clad pioneers were as deadly as the rattlesnakes they kicked out of their blankets, and as tough as the sixty bears a day they often saw. Their diseases—smallpox, for instance—killed far more red men than their rifles and knives. They drank and gambled away their money, seldom bathed, and often died as they had lived—violently.

When they had nearly exterminated the beaver, whose furs were sent east to be made into men's hats, the day of the mountain men was done. But, after their time, the passes and trails over the plateaus, peaks, and deserts had lost some of their mystery. The great West had given up many of its secrets to the mountain men, and the knowledge gained would be used by the tens of thousands of settlers who were later to travel trails the mountain men had blazed, following "the western star."

The Passing of the Spaniards

Los Californios

As early as 1800, Yankee merchant ships called at ports like Monterey and San Diego, trading everything from needles to plows for cattle products: hides, dried meat, and tallow. This traffic was smuggling, forbidden by Spain, but even the mission friars enjoyed it. The roads into Mexico were long and primi-

63

tive, and the *frailes* could not easily get needles and plows from New Spain. The ship captains bribed the port officials not to notice the illegal hides-and-tallow traffic, and everybody was happy. The first regularly employed Americans to become residents of California were ship agents for this illegal trade. Other Americans present—very few before 1846—were riffraff like ship deserters, fugitives from the law, and tramps. When the missions passed away, the *rancheros* of California continued the smuggling.

The carefree life of the *rancheros* inspired envy in the hearts of all who saw it or heard of it. With crude irrigation, the sunny land grew fruit and grain abundantly. Cattle, sheep, pigs, and goats roamed a countryside that was "like one continual pasture."

The California ranchers were illiterates who never walked a step if they could help it. Their books were few, but their

horses were many, and children rode from the day they could toddle. *Los Californios* were the finest horsemen in the world, either for acrobatics or endurance. At full tilt they could snatch off the heads of chickens buried to the neck in the ground. Or like Pío Pico, last Mexican commander in southern California, they thought nothing of galloping from San Diego to San Ga-

briel, 125 miles in one day, using relays of fresh mounts.

The men dressed in velvet trousers flared at the bottom and laced with gold. They wore loose, colored vests over bright shirts; red or black buckskin leggings; embroidered shoes; and big flat hats held on to their braided hair by leather straps. Their women dressed almost as gaily. Even the horses' saddles and bridles were decorated with gold, silver, and ribbons.

Someone had to pay for the lazy life of the *rancheros*. The Indians who did all the hard work died twice as fast as the Negro slaves in the American South. This sacrifice permitted the ranchers to pass their time visiting neighbors, dancing, and betting on cock- or bullfights. Doors were never locked, for there were no locks, and when a Californian said, *"Mi casa es suya,"* "My house is yours," he meant it. Sometimes, if he felt a guest needed money, he left a pile of coins on the guest-room table.

Some ranches covered enormous areas, up to forty-eight thousand acres. Ranch houses were built like the missions, often of adobe, with rooms opening onto a *patio* which had flowers and fountains. The Indians lived in single-roomed hovels.

Harried by revolutions at home, Mexico paid scant heed to governing California. During its first fifty years, only one of the republic's Presidents served out his full term. Yet anarchy in the motherland bothered Californians little until the death of honest Don José Figueroa, governor of California till 1835. Then corruption rioted in the province. Mexican governors came and went—at one time, four in a single year. The last, Don Manuel Micheltorena, turned up with a battalion of convicts for soldiers. The outraged *rancheros* threw him out, and obeyed no civil authority at all until the United States took over California in 1846.

66

New Mexico and Arizona

LIFE was much drearier in Arizona than in California. The fighting in Mexico during the 1820's drew off the soldiers who usually protected the province's farms and mines from marauding Yuma and Apache. Soon all but two of Arizona's towns and missions sheltered only lizards and owls. Walled Tubac and Tucson held out against the wrath of natives who long before had been taught by *conquistadores* like Coronado and Oñate to hate the white men.

New Mexico was the largest northern colony inherited from Spain by the Republic of Mexico. Forty-four thousand people

lived there, some very rich in sheep and silver, but most wretchedly poor. As in all Spanish colonies, there was no large or vigorous middle class. One reason the republic encouraged trade over the Santa Fe Trail was to raise New Mexico's standard of living.

Texas's First Boom

IN 1836, Sam Houston's old friend, President Andrew Jackson, warned him that he could not take Texas into the Union at once. Northerners protested adding another slave state, and some southerners feared a Texas that might fall under the domination of the federal government. The best Jackson could promise was recognition of Texas as a free republic—a recognition given on his last day in office in 1837.

In the next ten years, Texas's population boomed from 30,000 to 142,000. Most of the people came from the States, but many

Germans and others came from Europe. Corn, cotton, and cattle were the business of Texans, although the wild longhorns did not become profitable as meat until after the Civil War. Originally they were hunted for their hides, valuable for leather. Their meat was left to rot.

The immigrants brought with them the habits of home. By 1840 the north Texas country was sprinkled with schools, churches, newspapers, singing societies, and even a few amateur theater groups. An energetic new culture was overriding that of Spain and Mexico.

Black Beans and Statehood

MIRABEAU B. Lamar was a Georgian who had fought under Houston at San Jacinto. As second President of Texas, he subdued the Cherokee and Comanche and so eased the Indian dan-

gers to settlers. He also won recognition of Texas's sovereignty from England, France, and other powers. But Lamar could not dent Mexico's stern refusal to follow their example.

The Santa Fe Trail was open to Americans, but not to Texans. Lamar sent an expedition to Santa Fe to test Mexico's ban on Texans. Its members were captured and, hungry and freezing, were forced to march two thousand miles to Mexico City. Those who survived the death march were jailed.

Lamar's expedition had reminded the Mexicans that they ought to punish the upstart Texans. Twice they raided San Antonio, and once Corpus Christi. Sam Houston, President of Texas again in 1841, sent troops to retaliate, but with small success. Not only did most of the expeditions fail, but the men in one group, captured at Mier in northern Mexico, were told to draw beans from a jug. Those unlucky enough to draw black beans, one in ten, were promptly shot on Santa Anna's orders.

By now the United States no longer seemed cool to the idea of annexing Texas. "Manifest destiny" was carrying the day, and so was dislike of foreign interference. The United States was heading for a bitter Civil War only seventeen years away, but its North and South still could unite against arrogant European nations. In 1844, an Englishman swept away America's last hesitation about annexation. Lord Aberdeen proposed that England, France, and Mexico make Texas their protectorate and defend her against Yankee designs, by force if necessary.

This proposal enraged Americans who believed that the Monroe Doctrine had saved the Western Hemisphere from foreign meddling. President John Tyler saw that the time was ripe to add the Lone Star to the twenty-seven others on the flag of the Union. And Congress, led by men like Senator Benton of Missouri, passed a treaty of annexation. On July 4, 1845, the Texans ratified it with whoops of joy. On December 29, 1845, the newly elected President, James K. Polk, formally admitted Texas into the Union.

Six months later, the North felt happier to gain a free-soil area, Oregon, to offset slaveholding Texas. The Oregon Territory included the present states of Oregon, Washington, Idaho, and parts of Montana and Wyoming. Great Britain long had claimed

Oregon, but in the end gave it up peacefully by negotiation.

Carefree California was seized by the United States when war with Mexico started in 1846. A group of American settlers near the decayed mission at Sonoma had declared California to be a free nation, and ran up a homemade Bear Flag to prove it. (Some viewers thought the bear looked like a hog.) But another flag took over in July, 1846, when Commodore John Sloat hoisted the Stars and Stripes at Monterey, Mexican capital of California. At last the United States had fulfilled its "manifest destiny" by completing its Pacific boundary.

Cowboys and Tortillas
Names on the Land

FIVE western states have Spanish names: California, Colorado, Montana, Nevada, and New Mexico. Within them and neighboring states, hundreds of Spanish place names are religious, or somehow describe the locality.

El Paso's full name was El Paso del Norte, "the pass to the north"—into New Mexico from Old Mexico. The town of Alamogordo tells by its name that somewhere near there stood a stout poplar tree, an *alamo,* "poplar," *gordo,* "stout." Las Vegas says that towns with this name were surrounded by flat "plains" or "meadowlands." Some names seem queer, like Raton, "Mouse," Pass (so named for the many pack rats on the mountainside), or Punta Arguello, the "point of ill health." But perhaps the queerest of all is neither old nor Spanish. A few years ago the citizens of Sierra, New Mexico, changed their Spanish-named town to Truth or Consequences.

Religious names testify to the deep roots of Catholicism in Spanish life. The Sangre de Cristo Mountains, and the city of Santa Fe (de Cristo) honor the blood and holy faith of Christ. El Rio de las Animas Perdidas en Purgatoire, "the river of lost souls in purgatory," was too much of a mouthful for American cowboys. They cut it down to "Picketwire."

Anyone can pick out scores of San's and Santa's, male and female saints whose names bless places, rivers, and towns. San Diego (St. James) recalls Spain's patron saint.

73

Buckaroos and Vaqueros

OUR cowboys owe everything but their name and their hats to the Mexicans. "Buckaroo," from *vaquero* (cowboy), never caught on. And the *sombrero* lost out to a hat from Philadelphia

when the cowboys discovered that a Stetson not only shielded the head, but could be used to whip a bucking horse and could hold water without leaking.

Aside from these exceptions, the whole method and language of cow wrangling was invented south of the border. Texas and California styles of ranching differ, but their roping, branding, and working clothes all derived from the Mexicans. The American cowhand named his lariat from the Spanish *la reata,* "rope"; lasso from *lazo,* "noose"; quirt from *cuarta,* "whip"; ranch from *rancho;* stampede from *estampida;* and mustang from *mesteño,* "a stray." Another common English word, cinch, comes from *cincha,* "saddle girth."

Certain other Spanish expressions were muddled by American cowhands. Such is "vamoose," a corrupt form of *vamos,* "let's go," as "savvy" is of *sabe,* "know." Also, the cowboys called a jail a "hoosegow," from *juzgado,* "courtroom."

Today we all use words from the Spanish West: fiesta, rodeo, bonanza, mesa, alfalfa, corral, bronco, tornado, plaza, poncho, vigilante, burro, desperado, patio, sombrero, and canyon.

From the Kitchens of Montezuma

THE tomato is the most notable gift of the Mexicans and their Aztec ancestors to the world of cooking. Sixteenth-century Europeans thought "love apples," as they called tomatoes, were poisonous, and for a long time they hesitated to eat them. Another New World vegetable was maize, or corn, of which there were more than two hundred varieties in Mexico and Central America.

Barbecues are Indian, too. They were a common way of feeding hundreds of people at one sitting. Later, in Spanish California, whole steers seasoned with spicy barbecue sauces were roasted over pits full of hot coals, and served to the crowd.

What are called Mexican dishes usually are foods cooked as the Aztecs prepared them centuries ago. The flat corn pancake called a *tortilla* is basic. It may be eaten like bread, or rolled into sandwiches called *enchiladas* and *tacos,* filled with meat. *Tamales* are supposed to have saved the lives of Cortes' starving Spaniards, when the angry Aztecs of Montezuma's city of Tenochtitlán pelted them with these unlikely missiles.

And the Mexicans have raised the cooking of beans, *frijoles,* to a high art.

Avocados are still another Mexican donation to good eating. Easterners know them in salads, but westerners also know *guacamole.* It is a wonderful dip, spread, or dressing made from mashed avocados, chili powder, minced onion, lemon juice, and mayonnaise.

77

Figs, olives, dates, and oranges are not original to the New World, but their production in the Spanish-American West has helped make them common and inexpensive for the daily use of Americans all over the country. The same is true of fine wines, made from the beginning by the mission friars, who were California's first wine makers as well as first white settlers.

An odd story about food involves Don Mariano Vallejo, who worried about ways to increase the scanty supply of sugar in old California. Fruits, wines, and chocolate as a drink were the usual sweets. Vallejo wanted more plain sugar so badly that he even hired a man who claimed he could make sugar from beets. Don Mariano's friends thought he was slightly mad, and they howled at *El Azucarero,* "the sugar maker." *El Azucarero* did not succeed in producing sugar, but today raising beets for sugar is one of the large agricultural industries of the Spanish-American West.

The architecture of the missions and the early *ranchos* continues to be popular throughout the West, both in public buildings and private houses. In fact, the "ranch type" house has spread to all parts of the United States, although an old Don or friar might not be able to recognize most of these dwellings as of Spanish origin.

In many more subtle ways the imprint of Spain lingers in the American West. Deeds to real-estate properties may still bear the names of the original Spanish land grants, as in El Rancho de Corte Madera, a tract now covered by several small cities north of San Francisco. Corte Madera, "cut wood," used to furnish the San Francisco *presidio* with firewood.

Laws affecting mines, water rights, and the property shares of women date back to the Dons. The Roman Catholic Church

78

still claims the faith of millions of westerners and, for many, Spanish is their second language, if not their first.

The Spanish West now is the American West, but the lingering traces of the Dons, the friars, and the Indians give it a pleasant and distinctive flavor. And it is no wonder that the flavor remains, for the land was Spanish in character for more than three hundred years, while the United States has owned it for just over a century.

Index

81

DATE DUE

DEC 4			
GAYLORD			PRINTED IN U.S.A.